ZEAL

The Navigators is an international,
evangelical Christian organization.
Jesus Christ gave his followers
the Great Commission in Matthew 28:19 –
"Therefore go and make disciples of all nations."
The primary aim of The Navigators is
to help fulfill that commission by
multiplying laborers for Jesus Christ in every nation.

Korea NavPress is the publishing ministry
of The Korean Navigators.
Korea NavPress publishes books and materials
for the spiritual growth of Christians.
We help believers become committed disciples
of Jesus Christ and become laborers
who have mature character and leadership.

Originally published in Korean
as 열심 by 하진승.
Copyright © 1987, 2012 by Korea NavPress.
Translated into English by Jeremy Chen.

ZEAL

John Ha

TO KNOW CHRIST AND TO MAKE HIM KNOWN

Contents

Zeal 7

Why Must We Be Zealous 11

   1. Because God is zealous

   2. Because our Great Commission is extremely important

   3. Because zeal is God's will for His chosen people

   4. Because zeal is our motivation for victorious life

Zealous People in the Bible 25

How to Exert Zeal ································· 33

1. Live holy lives apart from sin
2. Walk in step with God
3. Have a personal conviction about the Great Commission

Training to Live with Great Zeal ··············· 61

1. Start with the little things
2. Be focused
3. Maintain the attitude of excellence
4. Rely on the Holy Spirit

ZEAL

I started doing evangelistic ministry in September, 1966. After twenty years of doing ministry, I got up one morning to reflect on the twenty years and thank the Lord for His blessings throughout that period of time. Then, I pondered to myself if God were to give me twenty more years to serve in the ministry, what kind of attitude should I have?

I thought, if I were to continue ministering for twenty years, I'd be a nearly seventy-year-old grandpa! Would I still be living at that time like I am living today? Would I be living in a lesser manner? Or would I be living in a greater manner than I am living today? As I mused about these possibilities, I had to think very seriously to myself. So I asked God in prayer, "In the next twenty years, how should I spend my days in order to live in the most worthwhile manner?" At the time, I thought of many things. What exemplified these thoughts the most was this: No matter how old I am, I must persist in being zealous. That is, to persevere in having an unquenchable fervency in my heart for the rest of my life. This included not knowing if I would continue to have good physical health, if I'd become a weak old man, or if I'd be stricken with illness, but no matter what happened, I desired in my heart of hearts to continue living with zeal. So I prayed that this would happen in my life.

God wants all people to come to salvation through our Lord Jesus, and He wants those who have received Him and become children of God to be living sacrifices before Him. Romans 12 urges those who have received Christ to start with such a mindset: "Therefore, I urge you, brothers, in view of God's mercy, to offer your bodies as living sacrifices, holy and pleasing to God—this is your spiritual act of worship" (Romans 12:1). There is a difference between offering your body as a living sacrifice and offering up what you have. Offering up one's body is to offer up everything that is associated with one's physical body. The kind of worship that pleases God doesn't consist of just offering up a part of what belongs to me in worship, but rather offering my very life. This is the kind of worship that God delights in.

But becoming a living sacrifice to God isn't a one-time emotional decision. In Romans 12:1 the apostle Paul exhorts us to offer our bodies as living sacrifices. In the following verses, he very specifically details what the lifestyle of one who has chosen to be a living sacrifice looks like. In verse 11, we are taught that one of the prerequisites of being a living sacrifice is zeal. "Never be lacking in zeal, but keep your spiritual fervor, serving the Lord"(Romans 12:11).

Consequently, if we lack zeal, it doesn't matter if we're doing Bible studies, attending conferences, listening to messages, or doing our quiet times. We won't be able to keep doing them for a lifetime. So we have to really let this sink in and think carefully about how to become a zealous Christian and how to become a fervent worker of His for a lifetime.

Why Must We Be Zealous

Before we look at how to live with zeal, let's first look at some reasons why we need to live zealous lives.

1. Because God is zealous

We should be zealous because the God we believe in, serve, and worship is zealous. Among God's many attributes and qualities, we need to study and learn His zeal. Isaiah 9:7 says, "Of the increase of his government and peace there will be no end. He will reign on David's throne and over his kingdom, establishing and upholding it with justice and righteousness from that time on and forever. The zeal of the LORD Almighty will accomplish this." This is to say that the LORD's zeal will fulfill His promises.

When someone produces a new work of art or makes a new discovery in science, people may have different opinions and judgments about it. Regarding the value of the new work or new discovery, most people are likely to depend on the experts' opinions and judgments about it. When it comes to all of creation, however, God is clearly the most accurate and just judge and the greatest authority of all authorities. The Scriptures mention that after God finished creating the whole universe, "God saw all that he had made, and it was very good.···"(Genesis 1:31). God values His own creation very highly. When we barely accomplish something, especially if we feel sluggish or hopeless at the time, it's hard to be satisfied with what we've achieved. We might sometimes even be ashamed. Even if we have the ability, if we fail to accomplish something due to our laziness, we most certainly feel ashamed. However, if we are highly motivated and zealous, when we accomplish something, we feel proud of ourselves and we feel a sense of accomplishment. One reason why the Almighty God can think so highly of His own creation is because His work of creation was done with utmost sincerity and zeal.

We must remember that in His work of creation, God didn't just use His almighty power; He used it with great zeal. Before the creation of the world, as God was making His plans, He must have considered with great zeal what He was going to create, how He was going to create it, in what order He would create it, where He should put it, etc. Having met a very high standard, God was very pleased with what He Himself had created. From the first day to the last, God carefully arranged every detail with all His heart and all His might. That is to say that from the very beginning up until now, God has been diligent and wholehearted in everything. He wasn't haphazard about anything, but diligent so that everything would be orderly and wonderful. It is obvious that God was very wholehearted in His work. In managing and guiding His creation, He is very zealous too.

He was likewise zealous in saving mankind from sin. "Again and again I sent all my servants the prophets to you. They said, 'Each of you must turn from your wicked ways and reform your actions.···'"(Jeremiah 35:15). For the sake of saving such rebellious sinners who were as enemies to Him, He sent many prophets and ambassadors, and finally even sent His own Son Jesus Christ to die for their sins. Through Isaiah God lamented, "All day long I have held out my hands to an obstinate people, who walk in ways not good, pursuing their own imaginations"(Isaiah 65:2). Because of this, he also cried out to the Lord, "O LORD, Your hand is lifted high, but they do not see it. Let them see Your zeal for Your people and be put to shame; let the fire reserved for Your enemies consume them"(Isaiah 26:11).

You see, God wasn't affected by how people ignored Him, but He was still zealous for them. In view of how great His zeal is, we are put to shame.

The apostle Paul imitated and lived out God's zeal. In his letter to the Corinthians, he said, "I am jealous for you with a godly jealousy. I promised you to one husband, to Christ, so that I might present you as a pure virgin to him"(2 Corinthians 11:2). In the midst of all the persecution and hardship, to not love one's own life but to persist in preaching the gospel and discipling others could only come from a clear understanding of God's zeal for His people. Furthermore, in his own life, God's concern for people became Paul's concern for people as well. His zeal wasn't to conform to any particular man's example, but rather a direct imitation of God's example, of God's zeal.

During His life here on earth, Jesus had the same kind of zeal. At the temple in Jerusalem, when He drove out those who were selling goods within the temple and cleaned up the temple courts, His disciples had a very deep impression and experience of His zeal: "To those who sold doves he said, 'Get these out of here! How dare you turn my Father's house into a market!' His disciples remembered that it is written: 'Zeal for your house will consume me'"(John 2:16-17). At that point, the disciples saw the Father's zeal through Jesus' actions: this experience was probably something that they remembered for the rest of their lives(see John 2:22). Do we remember God's zeal at all times? Because God is a zealous God, the kind of person that God is pleased with is a zealous person. He is also pleased with the sacrifices that such a person would offer. Thus, we should live lives full of zeal.

2. Because our Great Commission is extremely important

Once again, because the Great Commission

that God has entrusted to us is so important, we must be zealous. The Great Commission that God gave us is impossible to accomplish unless we have zeal. Our Lord Jesus said to His disciples, "Therefore go and make disciples of all nations, baptizing them in the name of the Father and of the Son and of the Holy Spirit, and teaching them to obey everything I have commanded you.⋯"(Matthew 28:19-20). No matter how hard people work, the Great Commission isn't something that can be accomplished by human strength. How would disciples of all nations be made and how would they be taught to obey everything that Jesus commanded? At the time, the disciples that heard these commands had no other resources other than the Commission itself. They didn't have broadcasting equipment, cars, radios, telephones, or offices. They didn't even have a single gospel tract! It's not as if the Lord Jesus didn't know this. Then how on earth could Jesus give these disciples who had next to nothing such a Commission?

The answer to this question is found in the "therefore." The significance of "therefore" is found in the Lord's preceding statement: "All authority in heaven and on earth has been given to me. Therefore⋯." We can see that all authority, not just in heaven, but also on earth, including today, belongs to our Lord Jesus Christ. It's not just some authority, but all authority. Thus, although we are weak and small, we can accomplish His Great Commission as we rely on the authority that has been given to our Lord Jesus Christ. However, God has promised that this authority is unleashed through zealous people whom He empowers. "For the eyes of the LORD range throughout the earth to strengthen those whose hearts are fully committed to him.⋯"(2 Chronicles 16:9). Consequently, when we are fully committed to God, we receive His power, and having received this power, we can accomplish the Great Commission that He has given to us.

Perhaps most of us have recognized that the

Great Commission is far more precious and meaningful than any other goal in life. But the key question is: would we still view this Commission as of utmost importance, even when we lose our reputation, our possessions, and all things that we hold dear? If we could keep our wealth, our name, and the pleasures of this life while completing the Great Commission, everyone would be willing. But if, in order to complete the Great Commission, you had to give up everything that you had, would you be willing to consider your own life worth nothing to you, as the apostle Paul did? Would you still be able to keep your zeal and fervor for the sake of completing the Great Commission?

To Paul, whatever was to his profit, he considered loss because of the surpassing greatness of knowing Christ. Also, for His sake, Paul had suffered the loss of all things, counting them as rubbish in order that he might gain Christ and be found in Him(see Philippians 3:7-9).

It is this kind of person that God wants today. God doesn't need a lot of lukewarm people, but rather people who, like the apostle Paul, have counted everything as loss, but are thoroughly convinced that the Great Commission is of utmost importance. At this very time, the eyes of the LORD are running to and fro throughout the whole earth, to give strong support to those whose heart is fully committed to Him.

3. Because zeal is God's will for His chosen people

Because one of God's purposes in saving us was to deliver us unto zealous living, we must live with zeal. Titus 2:14 says that Jesus Christ "gave Himself for us, that He might redeem us from all iniquity, and purify unto Himself a peculiar people, zealous of good works"(KJV). In order to make us a people zealous for good works, God saved us. Because God wants me, one whom He has saved, to always be zealous, I ought to live with zeal. It is my duty and it is the basis on which I must live my life. When we do something or buy something, we usually have some kind of purpose. But when we carry out that purpose, only then is the true value of what we have done or bought revealed. The purpose of an umbrella, for example, is to prevent rain from making us all wet. But the true value of the umbrella is not fully realized until it actually rains because that is when it is used according to its intended purpose. Accordingly, God saved us so that we could live with zeal. Consequently, all Christians should live with zeal.

When we live with zeal, a necessary result is a prosperous life. Hezekiah, king of Judah, was one who lived a very prosperous life. This is what the Bible records of him: "This is what Hezekiah did throughout Judah, doing what was good and right and faithful before the LORD his God. In everything that he undertook in the service of God's temple and in obedience to the law and the commands, he sought his God and worked wholeheartedly. And so he prospered" (2 Chronicles 31:20-21). Thus, a person who does all things wholeheartedly and who truly lives with zeal will have a prosperous life.

4. Because zeal is our motivation for victorious life

People who live with zeal don't stumble when they are tempted, but rather live victoriously. For a long time, King David lived a very devoted and fervent life. He was a very positive, but also very sacrificial and passionate person. But one day, he became lazy. When all of the troops had selflessly gone out to fight in battle, he went out for a walk on the palace rooftop. If there was one thing that he should do there, it should be praying earnestly for his troops, raising up his hands just like Moses did when Joshua was leading the Israelites in battle. It was his duty to do one of these: either to be praying earnestly for his troops or to be fighting in battle alongside them. But David didn't choose either of these. At that moment, he gave into his own desires. His eyes were filled with sinful desire as he looked to and fro, and then ultimately sinned.

Just as a running bicycle does not fall down, when we live with zeal, Satan won't be able to entice us to fall down to sin. But we must remind ourselves from time to time that when we are idle, Satan will certainly try to lure us into temptation. "Be self-controlled and alert. Your enemy the devil prowls around like a roaring lion looking for someone to devour"(1 Peter 5:8). We must constantly be self-controlled and alert, then, and zealously run along the path that God has marked out for us.

Zealous People in the Bible

Because of the reasons that we've discussed above, we should recommit to living a life filled with zeal. Let's then examine people that lived with great zeal in the Scriptures, so that we, too, can develop convictions for living with zeal as well.

Because God does all things with zeal, it only makes sense that God honors those who are full of zeal. Those that do not have zeal will not have His approval. In Revelation 3:16, God says, "So, because you are lukewarm—neither hot nor cold—I am about to spit you out of my mouth." The kind of person with whom God is pleased is first and foremost zealous.

God loved zealous Jacob. He was rather zealous about getting the firstborn's birthright. Throughout the book of Genesis, we observe that as a shepherd, he was both wise and passionate. When he was wrestling with the angel of the LORD, he was zealous to receive God's blessing, intent on wrestling until his body itself broke. He wrestled all night long pinning the angel to the ground, saying to him, "I will not let you go unless you bless me"(see Genesis 32:26). Consequently, Jacob was one who persistently sought after God's blessing until he finally got it.

In Judges 6, Gideon lived in a very dark time. During his time, Israel was in such hardship that she didn't have even a glimmer of hope. At that time, Israelites laboriously farmed, but when it was time for harvest, the Midianites would come and steal their crops. The Israelites would starve. In the midst of such terrible circumstances, Gideon didn't give up. If you look at Judges 6:11-12, we understand that when God called Gideon, he was beating out wheat in the winepress to hide it from the Midianites! God didn't speak to him while he was taking an afternoon nap, being idle, or playing around; instead, it was when he was diligently working in the midst of adversity that God called him to be used by Him.

In 1 Kings 19:19, we can see what Elisha was doing when God called him through Elijah: "So Elijah went from there and found Elisha son of Shaphat. He was plowing with twelve yoke of oxen, and he himself was driving the twelfth pair. Elijah went up to him and threw his cloak around him." God didn't call him while he was snoring away in the fields. He didn't appear to him in a dream. The Bible tells us that this calling didn't take place while he was being lazy, but instead while he was laboring away with twelve yoke of oxen. Can you imagine driving twelve yoke of oxen all at once? It's incredible!

In the midst of such zealous work, God called Elisha to be used of Him.

Furthermore, in 1 Kings 19:10, when Elijah was assessing his own zeal, he said that he had been very zealous for the Lord! It wasn't just that he had zeal, but that he was very zealous. Who would dare to say that way about themselves? But Elijah wasn't talking to himself; he was saying this in the presence of the Lord. It wasn't even in front of his disciples or other people, but it was to the Lord, the God of hosts, that he was offering this assessment that he had been very zealous for the Lord. Brothers and sisters, could you say that you have been very zealous for the Lord in His presence? If you were standing before other people, you might reluctantly say it, but if you were in God's presence, unless you were very confident that this were actually true, you wouldn't be able to speak like Elijah did. So Elijah had a positive attitude in living zealously, and he was thus able to say such a thing in the presence of God.

Additionally, in 2 Chronicles 19:4, we see a record of the life of King Jehoshaphat of Judah: "Jehoshaphat lived in Jerusalem, and he went out again among the people from Beersheba to the hill country of Ephraim and turned them back to the LORD, the God of their fathers." Jehoshaphat governed the territories frequently invaded by surrounding nations. This Jehoshaphat was a very spiritual man. But being a spiritual man, he didn't just sit and pray all day every day. Nor did he just rely on his words as a statesman. "Jehoshaphat lived in Jerusalem, and he went out again among the people⋯" Where did he go? "⋯from Beersheba to the hill country of Ephraim." Speaking in today's terms, he didn't just go to the capital or to prominent municipalities to speak with important leaders. He went all the way to the hill country of Ephraim. He went to talk to leaders of small clans and villages for the purpose of leading them back to the LORD, the God of their fathers. Was it because there weren't any prophets or priests at the time? As the king, he could have also commanded this or that person to go on behalf of the throne, but he didn't. He didn't just serve using his words. His great zeal inspired him to make his rounds in small towns and villages evangelizing in order to bring people back to God. This is the kind of zeal that we ought to imitate.

Another example of zeal is the apostle Paul, who, in Acts 20:20, said, "You know that I have not hesitated to preach anything that would be helpful to you but have taught you publicly and from house to house." The apostle Paul was a very famous man. He was a true gospel worker and laborer for the Lord, more famous than any famous Christian in today's day and age. But he didn't just evangelize at large group gatherings or at large evangelistic campaigns. It didn't matter if he was in front of a large crowd of people or inside a single person's home. No matter where he was or when it was, he would earnestly proclaim the Word of God without withholding anything. And it wasn't just in situations where things would go smoothly or when he was well prepared. As verse 19 tells us, he exuded zeal for the Lord through many hardships, tears, and trials. Actually, no matter where he went, some of his audience came to hear the Word of the Lord, but others came to persecute and ruin the apostle Paul as he taught the Word(consider Acts 17:13). So his great zeal was apparent not in situations in which he was well prepared or in which he got invitations left and right, but rather in situations of tears, suffering, and persecution.

Additionally, in Acts 20:24, Paul even described his own zeal by saying, "However, I consider my life worth nothing to me, if only I may finish the race and complete the task the Lord Jesus has given me—the task of testifying to the gospel of God's grace." He didn't say that he highly valued his own life, but that he considered his own life worth nothing to himself; he didn't even have to think about his own life a single bit. Why? It was because, to him, the gospel was more important than even his own life. Where on earth can we find people who don't appreciate their own lives? If most people, wanting to make a lot of money and subsequently making that money, were confronted by a robber demanding money, they would certainly choose to preserve their own lives. They'd say, "You can take all of my money, but don't kill me!" Would anyone say, "You can take my life, but please don't take all of my money away?" Of course not! Why is it that someone who spends a lifetime only concerned about money would still beg to save their own life? It is because people's lives are valuable. But the apostle Paul was convinced that sharing the gospel was more precious than life itself, so when he shared, he did so with great zeal.

How to Exert Zeal

In the previous sections, we have considered why we must have zeal, as well examples of great passion and zeal in the Bible. Now, let's consider questions such as, "Why don't I have zeal?", "It wasn't like this before, but how come I don't have much zeal right now?", and "How do I renew my zeal?"

1. Live holy lives apart from sin

The godly life that is set apart from sin is steadfast and can keep zeal alive in the heart. Sin robs zeal from our lives; sinning is like dumping water on top of a burning flame. When Adam was still sinless in the garden of Eden, he lived a life full of zeal. After He created all of creation, God gave all of the plants and animals on earth, in the oceans and in the skies to Adam and gave him dominion over all. Then, he also let Adam name all of the plants and animals. Naming things might sound easy, but it was a job that required careful consideration. When we name our cats, dogs, or other pets, we think about it for a long time. What about when we name a new business, shop, or product? Sometimes if you look at newspaper ads, you'll see electronics or car companies offering sums of money for people to suggest appropriate names for their products. Why would they do such a thing? This just shows how difficult it is to find an appropriate name. So choosing a name is a fairly complex process.

God entrusted Adam with such an important responsibility to name so many plants and animals; if he hadn't had great zeal or earnestness, he wouldn't have been able to complete this responsibility. For the purpose of completing his God-given task of naming all the creatures of the land, the birds of the air, or the fish of the sea, Adam earnestly pondered and worked day and night. Perhaps he categorized different plants and animals by their special characteristics, or perhaps like a scientist, he did different kinds of research to find the most appropriate name. In any case, he worked hard day and night to make sure that each plant and animal that he would govern in the future had its name.

But when he sinned, he lost the zeal that he had once had. From that time on, he didn't work busily to obey God's commands, but rather hid in the garden out of fear of being found by God. Brothers and sisters, have you ever thought of suddenly going into hiding? Haven't you ever felt like hiding yourself or stealing away somewhere as if you were chased by something scary? All of your zeal may seem to have vanished. What makes it happen? One of the main reasons is the problem of sin. Sin suppresses our confidence. Hebrews 12:1 says, "Therefore, since we are surrounded by such a great cloud of witnesses, let us throw off everything that hinders and the sin that so easily entangles, and let us run with perseverance the race marked out for us." So no matter how small our sin might seem to be, we must abandon it and cut it out of our lives.

But why do we sin? We must know the reason why we fall into sin, and be alert at all times. In order to better help us be set apart as holy and live out a holy life, we must be alert to consider the following:

a. We must be on guard against unbelief in God's Word

Often times, doubt doesn't come from ourselves, but is planted in our hearts by Satan. In Genesis 2:17, concerning the tree of the knowledge of good and evil, God said, "You must not eat from the tree of the knowledge of good and evil, for when you eat of it you will surely die." This is the unchanging Word of God. But in Genesis 3:4, Satan completely changes God's Word to its opposite, saying, "You will not surely die."

Just as it says in 2 Corinthians 4:4, Satan often blinds the eyes of our heart, causing us to doubt the Word of God: "The god of this age has blinded the minds of unbelievers, so that they cannot see the light of the gospel of the glory of Christ, who is the image of God." Satan hinders people from seeing the light of the gospel of the glory of God. Brothers and sisters, have you ever heard Satan's mocking voice that prompts people to doubt the Word of God? Am I truly saved? Does eternal life truly exist? Is the Great Commission truly of the highest value? Is the Great Commission truly more important than life itself? Will all of God's promises really come true? Is the spiritual multiplication the commission from the Scriptures? Is God's Word truth? Will Jesus really come again and judge, just as the Scriptures promise? Satan confuses us by keeping these doubts inside our hearts. Then, after these doubts are stored up one by one, we reject the authority of God's Word.

So the first step is to cause us to doubt the Word of God, and then the second is to undermine its authority. This way, when people do not acknowledge the authority of God's Word, they see their own opinions and discernment as that which truly has authority. Why are people stubborn, while they are repeatedly exhorted by God's Word? It is because they have elevated their own thoughts and discernment to the ultimate authority over God's Word. Then, when people elevate their own discernment to the ultimate authority, they fall into sin. Additionally, if they no longer see the Word as authoritative, they will lose all zeal for the Lord. In regard to my own attitude toward God's Word, which step am I at?

b. We must be on guard against a prideful heart

If a person comes to see God's Word as of the highest authority, then he will humble himself. If a person ceases to see God's Word as authoritative, he will fall into pride, which leads to a person wanting to become God. Even though he might not outwardly say he wants to become God, yet in his heart he cannot run from the thought that he is superior to God. Thus, he will become his own god and live according to his own desires. Adam didn't think that loving, worshipping, and praising God was a blessed and wonderful place to be in; instead, he wanted to be equal to God. When he had these thoughts, he lifted up his head in pride and saw as appealing that fruit which God had forbidden. When he became proud, he desired even that fruit which God so clearly forbade.

We are the same. Brothers and sisters, one day, you will realize your own pride. When you are proud, you can't even hear the admonitions of the brothers and sisters that you hold dear. You also can't hear the voice of your spiritual leaders who are constantly praying for you. You feel like you don't need to be exhorted. When a proud person is exhorted, he feels that those who exhort him are bothering him and dismisses their thoughts as inferior to his own. Not only does he ignore their exhortation, but also he runs to find those who will agree with his opinion. If someone has reached this stage, unless his pride is broken, exhortation from the Word will do him little good. So we must understand how terrifying it is to have a prideful heart, as it ushers us into further sin.

c. We must be on guard against a discontent heart

When God created Adam and Eve, He gave them everything. After God had finished creation, He saw all that He had made and it was very good. God was pleased with Adam and Eve, and He loved them, providing everything for them. As He watched them enjoy what He had made, He was filled with joy. As far as Adam was concerned, he had received God's greatest gift of grace and he had no other needs. He was acknowledged and encouraged by God, and all the blessing that he could receive from God was his. Under such circumstances, how could he lust for anything more? He should have been grateful and content with what he had. God forbade Adam from doing one thing, from eating fruit from the tree of the knowledge of good and evil. God gave him complete freedom in all things and allowed him to enjoy this freedom, but forbade him from just that one thing, but Adam still demanded from God, saying, "Give me freedom to do whatever I want." In doing so, he seized upon breaking God's only parameter and ended up falling into sin.

Our contemporary world is one of discontent. As we near the end times, our world has become discontent and ungrateful, just like the Bible tells us it would(see 2 Timothy 3:1-2). People will have what it takes to be content and yet nonetheless are not content. Many will exclaim, "Bless me!" or "Give me freedom!" but how much blessing and how much freedom would they consider to be enough? How much money would one need to have in order for him to consider himself wealthy? When a person is discontent with one thing, no matter how much grace, privilege, blessing, or freedom he is given, he won't see it. He can't see anything other than that which he covets and doesn't yet have. Are we like this? Have we counted our blessings from God, but still said to Him, "Lord, there's one thing that you haven't given me yet; please give it to me immediately" and then assumed a demanding attitude toward Him?

For a long time, the Navigators President Lorne Sanny had a dog. This dog had a strange habit; he'd dig holes in corners and under walls, not playing in open fields. He just wanted to get out. Lorne Sanny wanted to help him correct this habit of running away, but the dog just wouldn't comply. Are we sometimes like this dog? When we ignore the open fields that God has prepared for us, ones full of blessing, grace, and love meant for us to enjoy with gratitude, and instead are overcome by a heart that lusts after more and doesn't know how to be content, then we easily fall into sin. Before we count all the things that we don't have, we ought to count all the things that we do have.

When we pray together and one by one write down all the things that we already have, we quickly realize that to finish such a list is impossible! We have God, we have our Lord Jesus Christ who lives within us, we have eternal life, we have become children of God, we have become the bride of Christ, we are a royal priesthood, we are ambassadors for God, we have power, we have the fruit of the Spirit⋯ just to name a few! In addition, we have everything that we need from God on a daily basis. Why do we constantly count the things that we don't have?

Because of our excessive desires, we often fall prey to the same cycle of temptation and failure that Adam was subject to. When we doubt God's Word, become proud, and harbor discontent, our hearts become ungrateful. Adam wanted to take for himself that one thing which God prohibited and consequently sinned. The moment that he sinned, all of his spiritual fervor was immediately sapped from him. He became like a car without any battery left, so he hid himself. Such is a Christian who is deprived of his zeal. So an essential part of maintaining our spiritual zeal is, first and foremost, to throw off the sin. We must in all things have a thankful heart and a humble attitude, and let the Word of God fill our hearts to overflowing(Colossians 3:16, 1 Thessalonians 5:18).

d. We must be on guard against a spirit of comparison

There's a saying that goes, "The grass is greener on the other side." The result of comparing oneself with others is rarely positive. Most of the time, it's observing what I don't have that others do. This seems to be a very typical trait of human nature. You probably recall one of Aesop's fables. There once was a dog running across a bridge with a large bone in his mouth. When the dog saw his own reflection, he didn't realize that the reflection was of himself. He was envious of the big bone that the other dog had. Thinking of how to steal the bone for himself, he finally barked at the other dog, only for the bone that he himself had in his mouth to drop to the bottom of the river. When we are not content with what we have and are envious of what others have, it's easy for us to lose what we already have.

Typically, a comparing mind more easily develops in people who take initiative and are positive. When they are more in control of this comparing mind, because they know how to take initiative and are positive, they produce good fruit. But when they are unable to control this comparing mind, poisonous roots take hold of their heart and disturb its peace, frustrating them, leading them into sin, and quenching any spiritual fervor in their hearts. When Cain and Abel offered sacrifices to God, God accepted Abel's sacrifice, but did not accept Cain's. At this point, Cain did not come to the Lord in repentance, but rather compared himself with his brother, became angry, hated him, and then killed him. The reason why Saul wanted to kill David was also because of a spirit of comparison that was left out of control.

When Peter asked Jesus what the future held for the apostle John, the Lord resolutely said to Peter, "What is that to you? You must follow me!"(see John 21:19-23). Jesus was warning Peter not to let his concern for John devolve into a comparing mind. After hearing these statements, Peter must have turned back and worked diligently to uproot the comparing mind from within him. We, too, must examine ourselves in the presence of God rather than comparing ourselves with others. Frequently comparing ourselves with others can lead us to disappointment or even a sense of inferiority; it could also make us envious or jealous of others, leading to a root of bitterness and sin. Therefore, we must remain alert and carefully examine our own emotions so as to prevent a spirit of comparison from taking a hold of our hearts. This way, such a spirit of comparison wouldn't quench our zeal and cause us unnecessary struggles.

2. Walk in step with God

The resources necessary for a spiritual life are only found with God Himself, so it's to be expected that one would lose his zeal when he is not walking with God. Even one who is helping others as a spiritual leader could one day abandon his responsibilities if he is not truly walking with God; this can happen regardless of one's post or position. But one who is intimately relating with the Lord will keep the zeal unquenched. Having fellowship with God through the Word and prayer is like the roots to the tree of our spiritual lives. Through the Word and prayer, a person receives the strength he needs, bears fruit, and stands steadfastly. "So then, just as you received Christ Jesus as Lord, continue to live in Him, rooted and built up in Him, strengthened in the faith as you were taught, and overflowing with thankfulness"(Colossians 2:6-7).

When you think of "walking with God" in the Bible, the first person that comes to mind will be Enoch. How did he achieve the wonderful and amazing feat of persisting in walking with God? Some might think that Enoch grew up in an environment in which it was easy to walk with God. To the contrary, Enoch did not walk with God in a place that was comfortable, peaceful, or temptation-free, but in one of the most evil and depraved generations. Do you know the first song that was sung in the Bible? It wasn't one of praises to God. It wasn't a hymn. Rather, it was an evil and crazy song that glorifies cursing and exalts killers as heroes(see Genesis 4:23-24). Thus, Enoch lived in an era in which people were not ashamed of sin glorifying unrighteous men. Even so, there were many godly men belonging to the LORD during his day and age who were captivated by ungodly women and subsequently lost their spiritual fervor. So we see that Enoch lived during the time leading up to Noah and the flood. Isn't the spiritual condition of Enoch's age very similar to ours today?

Enoch walked with God for 300 years in this kind of environment. Some people might think that even though the time period when he lived was very difficult and sinful, his personal background might have been good enough to prepare him well to live a righteous life. But it wasn't as if Enoch had no family member to provide for. Nor did he live a very leisurely and carefree life or live as a hermit withdrawn from society. Nor did he stay in a quiet and cozy house reading the Scriptures, praying, or meditating all day. In today's day and age, Enoch would be an ordinary white-collar worker. He was also married and had kids. Enoch was a responsible parent, so he had to teach and train his children every day, sometimes even disciplining them. Basically, he was a diligent worker who was dedicated to providing for the needs of his family.

After Adam sinned, there were thorns and briers to deal with because the earth was cursed. According to Genesis 3:17, God said to Adam, "Because you listened to your wife and ate from the tree about which I commanded you, 'You must not eat of it,' cursed is the ground because of you; through painful toil you will eat of it all the days of your life." In Genesis 5:29, after Enoch's son Lamech became the father of Noah, he said, "He will comfort us in the labor and painful toil of our hands caused by the ground the LORD has cursed." This verse tells us how barren and infertile the land was. So it's incredible how Enoch, while pouring out blood, sweat and tears to work and take care of his family, was still able to walk with God. It was not in the midst of a very pleasant environment, but in one that was very similar to ours that Enoch was zealously walking with God.

For the sake of comparison, consider for a moment another Enoch, who is mentioned in Genesis 4:17. He was a son of Cain and a very successful man according to the eyes of the world. Sometimes we observe that cities, airports, or streets are named after a person. For example, Washington D.C., John F. Kennedy International Airport, or King Sejong Road are all named after a famous person. It's a pretty big honor to have something so important named after you. This is pretty much proof that you are well-known and revered. New Zealand's capital, Wellington, was named after the general who defeated Napoleon at Waterloo and later became prime minister of England. This kind of example is actually quite rare. However, coming back to Genesis 4, we see that Cain named a city after his son Enoch. What an honor this would have been to Enoch; from a very young age he had a famous reputation and was honored by many.

To the contrary, godly Enoch, the one who walked with God, had no such things to be proud about. He certainly poured out blood and sweat in his hard work. But it was not the one who had a city named after him that God loved. Rather God loved the one who walked with him through hardship and adversity, and continually gave him renewed strength. This godly Enoch didn't even face death but was taken up to heaven by God. Because he walked intimately with the Lord, he was able to live zealously for God over 300 years as one pleasing the Lord, and was blessed to immediately enter into His glory(see Hebrews 11:5).

Don't look for excuses in your environment. Don't say "Because I'm busy with my work⋯" or "Because I'm in the military service⋯" or

"Because I have to take care of the kids, it's hard to find time to commune with God. I can only spend seven minutes with God. Why do we have so many conferences, Bible studies, evangelism times, and meetings/gatherings of every kind? It'd be so nice if we only had to attend one meeting per a month." We shouldn't think like this. We've got to study the Word, pray, and have Christ-centered fellowship in order to spur one another on toward love and good deeds. We've got to share the gospel as part of our basic Christian life so that we can exude zeal in all that we do. Above all else, we must believe that our continuous, intimate fellowship with the Lord is what gives us living and active spiritual power in our lives. This is what drives us to enthusiastically pursue fellowship with God. "I rise before dawn and cry for help; I have put my hope in your word. My eyes stay open through the watches of the night, that I may meditate on your promises" (Psalm 119:147-148).

3. Have a personal conviction about the Great Commission

When the Great Commission that Christ has given to all believers becomes my own personal mission, then I can live with great zeal. If I believe that this Commission is set aside for some particular people, only those outstanding Christians or Christian organizations or churches, I cannot live a life of zeal. 'The Great Commission has been given to me, not to others. It is what I am personally obligated to do.' When we have the faith to receive the Great Commission, we can live a life brimming with zeal. We weren't called by God so that we'd look like good Christians in the eyes of others or so that we'd be avid participants in a Bible study. Our calling is also not just to be enthusiastically participating in Christian activities.

Each one of us has been called to serve the Lord in order to fulfill the Great Commission. God has called each of us so that the world may know Christ, that through Him they might receive all of His blessings, and that people of all nations would become his disciples. Our age, gender, family background, or intelligence have no bearing on whether or not the Great Commission applies to us. God has given the Great Commission to all people. But it's worth noting the only people who cannot fulfill it are those who are lazy. If a person has faith and zeal, he can accomplish the Great Commission. So if we brothers and sisters believe that the Great Commission is the thing that God cares most about, it goes without saying that we must focus all of our attention on it. Then, zeal will flow forth freely from our lives.

When one believes in the importance of the Great Commission, the zeal in his life might be seen in many different forms. For one, it might mean surrendering his whole life as an offering unto the Lord. For another, it might mean offering his finances to God. For yet another, it might mean laying down his reputation and status in order to suffer for the Great Commission. The apostle Paul was one such person who was recorded in the Scriptures as having laid it all down. He says, "But whatever was to my profit I now consider loss for the sake of Christ. What is more, I consider everything a loss compared to the surpassing greatness of knowing Christ Jesus my Lord⋯"(Philippians 3:7-8a). The apostle Paul also said that he forgot what was behind. Previously, he had done many things successfully, but he says that he chooses to forget all of these. We don't need to be admired by the world. In Christ, the things the world values are not so valuable after all, so we don't need to be disappointed that we are laying them aside. The Bible says that it is a foolish thing to be reluctant to part with what the world values, "as a dog returns to its vomit"(see Proverbs 26:11). It doesn't matter if we were successful or unsuccessful in the past; we've got to forget what is behind and press on toward the goal to receive the prize, as God through Jesus Christ beckons us. Only people who are certain of their goal and calling can display this kind of zeal in their lives.

Once in a while, I saw Olympic athletes practicing their sport on TV. Their bodies are covered in sweat, but they are committed to their sport with all their heart and all their strength. Why do they devote themselves to such difficult and strenuous exercises? What could possibly motivate them to do this? As the day of the competition nears, they leave their homes to train in earnest. Some of these athletes are already married. They leave behind their husbands and wives or even their children for this intensive training.

It's ironic that not many people would be willing to endure this kind of hardship for the purpose of spiritual training. For the singular goal of victory in competition, these athletes give their all in order to participate in the most intense training. How much bigger and more important is Christ's Great Commission than these

Olympic Games! The Great Commission that the Lord has entrusted to us is a goal that is greater than anything else on earth, but how shameful it would be to bring to our spiritual training and development anything less than the zeal that these Olympic athletes bring to their sport! As soldiers for Christ, we ought to all the more diligently and zealously prepare for the spiritual battles ahead of us. When new army cadets begin to train, we often hear this remark, "A drop of sweat in training is equivalent to a drop of blood in battle." This is a principle that can be applied directly in our spiritual lives. We must remember that a Christian's everyday life is a vigorous struggle with Satan.

"Everyone who competes in the games goes into strict training. They do it to get a crown that will not last; but we do it to get a crown that will last forever"(1 Corinthians 9:25). Think of how zealously athletes train, all for an earthly medallion. Since we want a glorious, eternal reward, how zealous should we be? Am I more committed than an athlete to what I have been called to? Have I been committed in the same way as an Olympic athlete that gives all that he has in order to get an Olympic medal? Once we have been convicted deeply of His Great Commission through His promises, all of our internal struggles will vanish, leaving only a pure, unadulterated zeal for God in our hearts. Then, the one who has such zeal has no worries. To him, everything is cause for rejoicing and thanksgiving because his heart is overflowing with praise. But when zeal is quenched, a person becomes fault-finding and is filled with resentment, struggles, complaints, and bitterness.

Training to Live with Great Zeal

Some people think that having zeal is just part of one's personality, but this is simply not true. When we take a close look at Jacob's life, he wasn't naturally an enthusiastic or zealous guy. He was a pretty quiet guy who preferred to stay at home, helping his mom in the kitchen with miscellaneous tasks. He seems to have been pretty shy or timid. His brother, on the other hand, was active and fiery, always running around hunting in the wild. But in regard to zeal to pursue blessings from God, they were the opposite. Jacob wrestled with God until dawn along the ford of Jabbok until his thigh-bone got dislocated; that's how zealous he was for obtaining the Lord's blessing. We, also, must be more zealous in pursuing spiritual blessings from God. Even though Esau's personality was active and fiery, because he didn't really care for the blessing—much less have zeal for it—he ended up missing out on it. So personality doesn't have much bearing on one's zeal for the Lord, nor can we use it as an excuse for why we aren't zealous.

Zeal isn't part of innate personality, but it is part of character that is developed and trained. Furthermore, the zeal that we are seeking and pursuing isn't the kind that engages in worldly busyness, but is zeal for God Himself and zeal for living a godly life. In 1 Timothy 4:7-8, God commands us to train ourselves in godliness. In order to obey this command, we must understand that zeal must be trained as part of our character; this is non-negotiable. If we want to live according to God's Word, then we must imitate His zeal. Zeal for godliness isn't given to us naturally; it is rather developed through training. Let's think about a few things we should remember if we want to train in having godly zeal.

1. Start with the little things

Training in having godly zeal is just like all other training. It's easy to give up if you start with too lofty a goal. Thus, when we first start training, we have to start with zealously executing small tasks.

For example, if I want to spend quiet time with God in the morning, then I've got to start small as well. I can start with seven minutes of reading and meditating on a short passage, punctuated by prayer. Then, I can train myself to gradually increase to fifteen minutes, then thirty minutes, or maybe even an hour. For memorizing scripture, I can start with a few basic verses. When these verses have become mine, then I can start to memorize the topical memory system verses and so on.

2. Be focused

We've got to start training with smaller tasks and then prayerfully obey that which we have learned. We must focus our attention on what the Lord has convicted us of. When we don't focus on one thing, we may become distracted or lazy, a surefire strategy for quenching spiritual zeal. Busily scurrying from one activity to the next doesn't make us zealous people. If we have divided attention in doing many things and don't have much to show for our investments, we may actually feel even more frustrated. As soon as we decide to start something, then we must focus and persevere until we complete it.

Have you heard the story of a mother who called her son who was about to go picking raspberries? "Sweetie," she said, "when you go to pick raspberries, don't look at the other children running from place to place looking for raspberries. Just pick a place and stick to your bush." This little boy listened to his mom. When he and the other children got to the part of the mountain with raspberries, he went to work at picking raspberries. After picking raspberries for some time, he looked at another bush that appeared to have even more raspberries. The other children were noisily running from bush to bush. The little boy wanted to run around just like the other children, but, remembering the words of his mother, he stayed in place. He diligently stuck to his position and picked raspberries until he had picked all the raspberries to be seen. Then, he moved on. Other children kept moving around from place to place after only picking raspberries for a little bit. When it was time to leave the mountain, the little boy discovered that his basket had more raspberries than the baskets of the other children and he was very pleased. Not only did the other children have fewer raspberries, but also in their haste, they had picked many rotten raspberries, with a lot of chaff mixed with the raspberry leaves. He also saw that the other children were very tired.

When we do things, it is worthwhile for us to heed the advice of that boy's mother. Brothers and sisters, when it's time to memorize a verse, focus on doing that. When it's time to fellowship with others, focus on doing that. When we are communing with God in the mornings, we've got to wholeheartedly and attentively listen to His Word and pray. If we have our Bibles open in front of us, but we're distracted by our responsibilities for the day or by other thoughts, we shouldn't expect to have much zeal for the day. If we are in the presence of the living God and yet are diverting our attention to other things, how can we expect to be zealous for Him?

This is what James warns us of: "That man should not think he will receive anything from the Lord; he is a double-minded man, unstable in all he does"(James 1:7-8). What this passage is warning us of is that when we halfheartedly do things, we can accomplish nothing and cannot expect God's help.

The effect of our keeping focused is like that of a magnifying glass. A magnifying glass can take plain sunlight and burn up a piece of paper or even start a large fire. In our lives, if we focus on doing something, our focused attention can bring about a significant change, no matter what it is we are focusing on. When we can train and develop our ability to do anything and fully devote our body, soul and spirit to attentively carry it out, then we can fulfill the Lord's command to "Love the Lord your God with all your heart and with all your soul and with all your mind and with all your strength"(Mark 12:30). Much training and development can be seen in a person who has such a heart, a heart that is completely devoted to do each, individual thing unto completion.

3. Maintain the attitude of excellence

When we are training our zeal, one thing that we cannot go without is an attitude of wanting to do all things excellently. When we are cleaning the house, washing clothes, arranging tables, combing our hair, managing household appliances and tools, etc., even in such mundane everyday activities, our insistence upon doing things excellently can carry over to our spiritual lives, enabling us to further exhibit spiritual zeal. It is worth clarifying that when I refer to doing things excellently, I'm not talking about the skill or ability level of a person(which may vary), but about his heart posture. When we paint our homes, our skill level may not be as good as a professional painter, but our sincerity and zeal could certainly exceed that of a professional painter. Needless to say, if we have this kind of attitude, our skills and abilities could develop as well! "Whatever you do, work at it with all your heart, as working for the Lord, not for men"(Colossians 3:23). May you work diligently in such a way that when you have finished, you would see that what you have accomplished is very good.

4. Rely on the Holy Spirit

"Not that we are competent in ourselves to claim anything for ourselves, but our competence comes from God"(2 Corinthians 3:5). In all training, any good progress is from God. Training in godly zeal doesn't just depend on our decisiveness or hard work, so we must rely on the Holy Spirit. Our Helper and Comforter is always with us, teaching us, reminding us, helping us in our weakness, guiding us(see John 14:26). So we must continually be sensitive to following the prompting of the Holy Spirit and be diligent in our training.

Some people misunderstand the promptings of the Holy Spirit. For example, they don't have a heart that wants to share the gospel or they don't share when they don't feel like it. Then, they attribute these attitudes to the Holy Spirit. But this is just following feelings, as these are not of the Holy Spirit. God has already instructed us that we should be ready to preach the gospel in season and out of season. The Holy Spirit speaks in accordance with the commands of the Word of God; He will certainly not contradict God's revealed Word. The Holy Spirit would say that we must preach the gospel at all times, wherever we go. Being zealous is also one of His commands: "As many as I love, I rebuke and chasten: be zealous therefore, and repent"(Revelation 3:19, KJV). When we don't feel like preaching the gospel, we should muster up our courage to go preaching. When we don't feel like reading the Bible, after praying, we should crack open our Bibles and start to read. Then the Holy Spirit gives us a fresh attitude, a new heart, and a living motivation. Even when our heart inclines to be lazy, if we obey God's Word and overcome this to be zealous, the Holy Spirit will bless us tremendously and change our hearts.

✶ ✶ ✶ ✶ ✶

Because we live in a generation that is more crooked and depraved every day, we must pay close attention to ourselves, lest our zeal grow cold. In the winter, when the temperatures get colder, we must burn fuel to an even hotter temperature. In the same way, as the world gets more evil and corrupt, we must be even more zealous for our God.

It should come as no surprise that the generation in which we live is referred to as the end times; that is to say that the Lord will come again soon. Nevertheless, people say that we shouldn't be so concerned with the Lord's second coming, but that we should be more concerned with what is happening in today's day and age. Talking about the world today may be important or sometimes even necessary, but it's not necessarily as urgent or as important as preparing to receive Jesus when He comes again.

We must claim and hold onto our Lord Jesus' promise of "Yes, I am coming soon!"(Revelation 22:20), and we must live a life in light of His second coming. So what kind of person should we become today?

> *Since everything will be destroyed in this way, what kind of people ought you to be? You ought to live holy and godly lives as you look forward to the day of God and speed its coming. That day will bring about the destruction of the heavens by fire, and the elements will melt in the heat.*
>
> *2 Peter 3:11-12*

There is no time to hesitate or delay. Nor can we shrink back or be lukewarm. Just as God exhorted the Laodicean church, we must be zealous and repent(see Revelation 3:14-22)! Are we today like the Laodicean church, neither cold nor hot, but only lukewarm? To say it another way, do we realize that we are wretched, pitiable, poor, blind, and naked, even while we say that we are rich, we have prospered, and we need nothing? Don't you feel that you don't need the teaching, reproof, and training of others because of your material wealth, because of your own thoughts, opinions, or stubbornness, or because of a futile superiority complex? Now is the time to see yourself as God sees you, and to turn back to Him so that you can once again be full of zeal for Him. Because God loves us, He rebukes, disciplines, and exhorts us.

As many as I love, I rebuke and chasten: be zealous therefore, and repent.
Revelation 3:19, KJV

Personal Application

1. What are some factors that motivate me to be zealous? List three in order of importance.

2. In my life, in what areas do I need to be more zealous? List them below and make specific obedience plans in one or two of the areas.

3. What things hinder me from being zealous for God? What measures can I take now to avoid these hindrances?

ZEAL

Copyright ⓒ 2018 by Korea NavPress

Korea NavPress
16 Yeonhuiro, Sudaemungu, Seoul 03784
http://navpress.co.kr

ⓒ All rights reserved.
No part of this publication may be reproduced
in any form without written permission
from Korea NavPress.

ISBN 978-89-375-0558-4   02230

First printing, 2018
Printed in Korea